Littlest Pet Shop

THE NIGHT BEFORE CHRISTMAS

By D. Jakobs
Based on the poem "Visit from St. Nicholas" (1823) by Clement C. Moore.
Illustrated by Jim Talbot

SCHOLASTIC INC.

New York   Toronto   London   Auckland   Sydney
Mexico City   New Delhi   Hong Kong   Buenos Aires

ISBN-13: 978-0-439-91906-7
ISBN-10: 0-439-91906-1

12 11 10 9 8 7 6 5 4 3 2 1   7 8 9 10 11/0

Printed in the U.S.A.
First printing, October 2007

It was the night before Christmas,
and all through the shop,
the pets did not stir,
or scamper, or hop.

The stockings were hung by the hamsters with care, in hopes that St. Nicholas soon would be there.

The pets were nestled all snug in their beds,
while visions of yummy food danced in their heads.

A Maltese in her ribbons and Scottie in his cap
laid their heads on their paws for a long winter's nap.

Then out in the street, there was such a clatter,
Scottie sprang from his bed to see what was the matter.

To the window he ran, fast as a pup.
He did not bark; he did not wake his friends up.

He stared out at the view of the snow and the stars,
lit up all around by the glow from the cars.

With a little old driver, so lively and quick,
he knew in a moment it must be St. Nick.

But what he saw next took his breath away—
it was eight tiny pets pulling a miniature sleigh!

As they flew closer and closer like jets,
St. Nick called out to his flying pets:

"Now, turtle! Now, kitten!
Now, shih tzu and monkey!"

"To the side of the street!
To the front of the door!"

"Now dash on in! Dash on in!
Dash into the store!"

With a bark, Scottie hopped around on all fours,
then hurried over to wait by the door.

When the door opened, as wide as a grin,
those magical pets, they came right on in.

In pranced and hopped each little paw,
or flew in or scuttled each little claw.

St. Nick had a bundle of toys on his back.
It was bulging and full—a very plump sack!

His eyes—how they twinkled!
His face, oh so merry!
His cheeks were like roses,
his nose like a cherry!

His cute little mouth was drawn up like a bow,
and the beard on his chin was as white as the snow.

He had a sweet face and a round little belly
that shook when he laughed, like a bowl full of jelly.

He was chubby and plump, a right jolly old elf.
Scottie barked when he saw him, in spite of himself.

With a wink of his eye and a tap of his feet,
St. Nick tossed Scottie a sweet little treat.

Scottie gobbled it up with a soft bark of joy,
while St. Nick chuckled and said, "My, what a good boy!"

Then without another word, St. Nick delivered the toys,
and his friends all helped out with barely a noise.

He gave Scottie a friendly pat on his snout,
and with a small wink, he led the way out.

Scottie watched from the door as he sprang to his sleigh, and away they all dashed without any delay.

But Scottie heard him exclaim,
as he drove out of sight . . .

MERRY CHRISTMAS

**to pets, and to pets
a good night!**